MW00613152

Successfully Writing the GED Extended Response

It's EASY when you understand what to do!

Copyright

© 2015 by Christina Mutch. All rights reserved. No part of this document may be reproduced or transmitted in any form or by any means, electronic, mechanical, photocopying, recording or otherwise, without prior written permission of Christina Mutch.

Dedication

For Mom and Dad who decades ago said to go to college and be a teacher, because there would always be a need for them. Who knew that I would grow to love my profession.

For eljase, a great friend. Thanks for continuing your expertise in the world of computer graphics and making this book cover.

To my students who by reading and understanding this book passed their GEDs, You are now onto a brighter, more prosperous future.

If this book helps you learn to write the GED extended response, I invite you to leave a review that might assist others. You may also contact me at my webpage; www.cmmutch.com

Successfully Writing the
GED Extended Response

Table of Contents

Successfully Writing the GED Extended Response

Then and Now

Several years before the 2014 GED, I wrote an instructional book called "Successfully Writing the GED Essay" for my adult education students. It laid out how to write, clearly and concisely, the GED essay. It not only proved to be a great help in brainstorming ideas for what students wanted to write, but it also laid out a simple process for writing the GED essay. The essays prior to 2014 were also much shorter and they were based on personal opinion. When January 2014 rolled by, I thought that book was no longer a valid guideline for the GED since the writer now had to compose an objective, argumentative essay that was substantially longer and more complex. I was wrong; the basics remain the same.

So to start, just what is an argumentative essay? Well, it's something like a 'debate' and you need to choose a side. The article presents opposing points of view of a given issue, or it might present contrasting views of two authors. Your job is to read the article then pick a side to support.

What is different in the 2014 GED Extended Response from the prior version of the GED essay?

- First off, your opinion is not wanted. That means **no** "I think," "I feel," "You should," etc. The essay is to be from an objective point of view based on the article; meaning you stay in third person. (ie) *the author, the article,* or *he, she, it, they, them, their, someone, anyone,* etc.

- You are to deal strictly with the facts presented in the article. You cannot add information that is not already presented. The extended responses are also expected to be longer than previous GED essays. *The limit to this one should be around 900 words. The only reason for that limit is test-takers are likely to run out of time if they are any longer in length.*

- Here is the most important thing you need to do. You must use facts from the article to back up the remarks you write down in your essay. If you do not do this, the GED grading system considers you are <u>listing</u> things and not discussing or analyzing the pros and/or cons of the article. Doing that could get you a '0' score. You need to find backup in the article to support your remarks. That backup can come in the form of quotes or paraphrasing (putting the quote into your own words.)

When you write your essay, try to use the following suggestions:

- Be sure to determine which position presented in the passage(s) is better supported by evidence from the passage(s).

- Explain why the position you chose is the better-supported one; remember the better-supported position is not necessarily the position you agree with.

- Defend your statements with multiple pieces of evidence from the passage(s).

- Build and support your main points as clearly and completely as you can.

- Put your main points in logical order, and tie your details to your main points.

- Carefully organize your response and consider your audience, message, and purpose.

- Use transitional words and phrases to connect sentences, paragraphs, and ideas.

- Carefully choose your words in order to express your ideas plainly.

- Watch your spelling. If you think of a word but do not know how to spell it, then use another word.

- Vary your sentences to help the flow and clarity of your response.

- Reread and revise your response to correct any errors in grammar, usage, or punctuation.

Grasping these steps will go a long way in helping you successfully write a 2014 GED Extended Response.

It is also important for you to remember that the first essay you write will be hard, because you are unsure what you should write or how the essay should go together. If you are going to use this book, when you finish an essay, take it to an English teacher or someone well versed in writing argumentative essays and go over it together. You will learn what and where your strong points are and where you need to make changes. After you have completed a couple essays, you will feel more comfortable writing them because you will understand what is required and expected from a successful GED Extended Response.

A suggested timeframe for the 45 Minute RLA Extended-Response Essay

- Read the article several times – 10-15 minutes

- Writing the 1st draft of the essay – 20 minutes

- Revise and Editing of the essay – 10 minutes

Another thing to remember is that once you begin this portion of the test, you cannot go back to answer any previous language questions, so take every minute you can on this.

The Extended Response

Who Is the Greater Superhero: Spiderman or Captain America?
(The Prompt and the Article)

Before starting the introduction, let's read the article from which the essay will be written. I chose Spiderman and Captain America because so many of my students were familiar with these characters.

Prompt - *Every superhero has abilities and assets that were acquired either before or after the change that made him a superhero. In your response, analyze the abilities and assets of both Spiderman and Captain America to determine who the greater superhero is. Use relevant and specific evidence from the article to support your response.*

Spider-Man

Spiderman's (aka Peter Parker) abilities and assets are used to combat his many foes. He receives most of his abilities when he is bitten by a lethally irradiated spider. It caused body-wide changes: primarily superhuman strength, reflexes, balance and the ability to cling tenaciously to most surfaces; and a subconscious precognitive sense of danger. This is called his "spider-sense," and one of its aspects manifests in a tingling feeling at the base of his skull alerting him to personal danger in proportion to the severity of that danger.

Spiderman's overall metabolic efficiency has been greatly increased; the composition of his skeleton, connective tissues, muscles, and nervous system has all been enhanced. His vision became 20/20, allowing him to see perfectly without his glasses. Spiderman's healing ability is more extensive, and he is capable of healing from injuries as severe as broken bones within a matter of hours.

Spiderman has conscious control over crawling on walls and ceilings. He can also use his clinging ability to lift or hold objects; for instance, he can catch a thrown ball simply by touching it with one fingertip. Spiderman is also able to jump and sprint along a wall, which helps him climb surfaces a lot faster.

Spiderman's agility and reflexes are far superior to those of an ordinary human, even those that represent the peak of human conditioning. The speed of his reflexes combined with his spider-sense allows him to dodge almost any attack, even point-blank gunfire. Spiderman has the ability to maintain his equilibrium when sticking to any surface.

Before becoming Spiderman, Peter Parker was already knowledgeable in chemistry, physics, biology, engineering, and mathematics, which he utilized in his Spiderman persona to develop his webbing. When he swings across a city on his web lines, his spider-sense guides his aim allowing him to travel at high speeds hundreds of feet above street level with minimal concentration.

Captain America

Captain America is the alter ego of Steve Rogers, a frail, young man who was enhanced to the peak of human perfection by an experimental serum in order to aid the United States government's efforts to win World War II. Captain America has no superhuman powers, but through the Super-Soldier Serum and Vita-Ray treatment, he is transformed and his strength, endurance, agility, speed, reflexes, durability, and healing are at the zenith of natural human potential. The formula enhances all of his metabolic functions and prevents the build-up of fatigue poisons in his muscles giving him endurance far in excess of an ordinary human being, including running a mile in 73 seconds at 49 mph. Rogers' body regularly replenishes the Super-

Soldier Serum; it does not wear off.

He is highly resistant to hypnosis and gases that could limit his focus. He has blended judo, western boxing, kickboxing, and gymnastics into his own unique fighting style, and he is a master of multiple martial arts. Years of practice with his near-indestructible shield make him able to aim and throw it with almost unerring accuracy. His skill with his shield is such that he can attack multiple targets in succession with a single throw or even cause a boomerang-like return from a throw to attack an enemy from behind. Captain America wears a costume that bears an American flag motif.

Rogers' intelligence and stratagems stem from vast US military knowledge, battle experience and training. This makes him an expert tactician and an excellent field commander, and with his shield, he is nearly unbeatable.

After Rogers becomes Captain America, he is often shown to be familiar with ongoing, classified Defense Department projects and Special Ops. He is an expert in combat strategy, survival, acrobatics, military strategy, piloting, and demolitions.

Putting Together the Brainstorm

Brainstorming is always the best place to start, especially in an essay. When you brainstorm, look for the action verbs in the prompt. Those will tell you what the prompt is asking for. If you look at the prompt below, the verb phrases tell you what you need to do.

Prompt: *Every superhero has abilities and assets that were acquired either before or after the change that made him a Superhero. In your response, <u>analyze the abilities and assets of both Spiderman and Captain America</u> to <u>determine who the greater superhero is.</u> <u>Use relevant and specific evidence</u> from the article to support your response.*

From the underlined verb phrases, the prompt is telling you to <u>analyze</u> the abilities and assets of each Superhero. (After seeing the comparisons, an introductory paragraph for this essay will be provided.) Before you can begin an essay like this, you need to brainstorm (write down) the abilities, intellect, or proficiencies of what needs to be analyzed or compared.

The next few pages will show you what a brainstorm comparison might look like. The first paragraph will focus on **abilities** and the second will look at their **intellect.**

	Spiderman	**Captain America**
1st Body Paragraph *Compare and analyze __abilities__ in the same paragraph.* *Pull evidence from the article to support your claims as either quotes or paraphrasing.*	Spiderman received abilities when he was bitten by a radioactive spider. Some of them are: - superhuman strength, reflexes and balance - ability to cling to most surfaces - injuries heal in hours *(Refer to evidence from article to support your remarks)*	The Super-Soldier Serum enhanced Captain America's metabolic functions. Some of them are: - his endurance, strength, agility, speed, and reflexes to the peak of human potential permanently - he is resistant to gases and hypnosis - he can run a mile in 73 seconds - injuries heal in hours *(Refer to evidence from article to support your remarks)*
2nd Body Paragraph *Compare and analyze __intellect__ in the same*	As Peter Parker, Spiderman was already very intelligent. He understood and excelled in: - chemistry, physics, biology - engineering - mathematics - his knowledge of science	As Steve Rogers, Captain America had knowledge of: - US military tactics - combat strategy and demolitions - training that made him an expert tactician and field

| *paragraph.* *Pull evidence from the article to support your claims as either quotes or paraphrasing.* | created his webbing A main asset is his subconscious foreseeing sense of danger; this is called his 'spider sense'. It also guides him. Another is his webbing to swing from building to building | commander - knowledge of judo, western boxing, kickboxing and gymnastics, and after becoming Captain America, he blended them into his own fighting style - he is also a master in multiple martial arts A main asset is his near-indestructible shield that can be used defensively or thrown as a weapon |
| | *(Refer to evidence from article to support your remarks)* | *(Refer to evidence from article to support your remarks)* |

This type of brainstorm makes comparisons and analyzing easier to see as well as to determine what to write. Note, I have made two comparisons, but you can have three. The comparisons are the abilities/enhancements the men received after becoming superheroes, and the second compares what is unique about them and the intellectual assets they possessed before and after becoming superheroes.

Writing the Introduction

The next step, after reading the article 2 or 3 times, is to write the first paragraph of the GED Extended Response. This paragraph is the <u>introduction</u>. Reading the article more than once will help you become more familiar with it and help you decide what viewpoint you want to support.

A good introductory paragraph should include:

- <u>Rewriting the prompt</u> in your own words; this will make the process much easier.

- Stating which side of the argument you are going to support.

Here is an example of an introductory paragraph that will present the two brainstormed ideas from the previous page.

Captain America and Spiderman are both Superheroes. Both had superior talents and assets before they became Superheroes, and others that were enhanced after their change. Both superheroes also possess abilities that are unique to them, but the evidence shows Captain America's talents and assets outweigh those of Spiderman. (I have rewritten the prompt in my own words using 'assets' instead of 'intellect'; however, assets defined means a useful or valuable quality. Finally, I have stated which view I support. Note that I did not use 'I,' 'me' or 'my' in this paragraph. I am keeping everything 'third person' objective.)

Stating the Main Idea through a Thesis Statement

Okay, now let's look at the above example and see what has been presented. The *main idea* sets the **tone** (which is the mood and meaning) for the essay. The *thesis statement(s)* are what you are going to talk about. It is here the information to be presented is addressed.

Essay prompt:

Every superhero has abilities and assets that were acquired either before or after the change that made him a Superhero. In your response, analyze the abilities and assets of both Spiderman and Captain America to determine who the greater superhero is. Use relevant and specific evidence from the article to support your response.

Main idea:

Who is the greater superhero?

Introductory paragraph with Thesis statements that are underlined:

Captain America and Spiderman are both Superheroes. <u>Both had superior talents and assets before they became Superheroes, and others that were enhanced after their change. Both superheroes also possess abilities that are unique to them,</u> but the evidence shows Captain America's talents and assets outweigh those of Spiderman.

What's In the Body?

The second, and longest section of an essay, is the body. The first body paragraph is going to discuss the first brainstormed point: Spiderman and Captain America's abilities and what they are.

Spiderman	Captain America
Spiderman received abilities when he was bitten by a radioactive spider.	The Super-Soldier Serum enhanced Captain America's metabolic functions.
Some of them are: (these are an overview)	Some of them are: (these are an overview)
- superhuman strength, reflexes and balance	- his endurance, strength, agility, speed, and reflexes to the peak of human potential permanently
- ability to cling to most surfaces	- he's resistant to gases and hypnosis
- injuries heal in hours	- he can run a mile in 73 seconds
	- injuries heal in hours
(Refer to evidence from article to support your remarks)	*(Refer to evidence from article to support your remarks)*

Remember, even though you are looking at both Spiderman and Captain America's abilities after they 'went through their change,' the analysis/comparison will comprise one paragraph. There is no limit as to how long or short the paragraph is, but you must compare/analyze their abilities in a single paragraph. That means you are going to bring up the radioactive spider bite that made Peter Parker Spiderman and the enhancements of his reflexes, strength and balance as well as his ability to cling to surfaces and sense danger, and heal from injuries in hours. In addition, you are going to use information from the article in either quotes or paraphrasing to give evidence of these changes.

You are going to do the same thing for Captain America. You are going to discuss the Super-Soldier Serum and Vita-Ray that made Steve Rogers into Captain America, and you will use evidence from the article to support your discussion of his enhanced strength, healing, agility and reflexes, immunity to gases and his ability to run a mile in seconds.

To restate once again, this is an analyzation/comparison between the two superheroes that will be accomplished in one paragraph.

You do not need to restate whom you chose as the greater superhero; that will happen in the conclusion.

Here is an example of what a first body paragraph might be. Remember to pull evidence from the article to support your claims as either quotes or paraphrasing.

Spiderman, aka Peter Parker, acquired his abilities when he was unexpectedly bitten by a radioactive spider. The result of the bite gave him superhuman strength, reflexes and balance. His overall metabolic efficiency was greatly increased, and the "composition of his skeleton, connective tissues muscles and nervous system" were all enhanced until he could dodge almost any attack including "point-blank gunfire." Because of the spider bite, Parker became more spider-like and could crawl across walls and ceilings with fingers and feet that clung to most surfaces. Another benefit is his ability to heal from injuries, including broken bones, within hours. During World War II, Steve Rogers became Captain America because he volunteered to be injected with the "Super-Soldier Serum" and be exposed to a "Vita-Ray." It was an experiment meant to aid the US in its efforts to win the War; the result of these treatments caused Rogers' body to be enhanced to the "peak of human perfection." Though as Captain America, Rogers has no super powers like Spiderman, his strength, endurance, agility, speed, and reflexes were heightened to the "zenith of natural human potential." His new metabolic functions prevented him from feeling fatigue and increased his endurance until he far exceeded ordinary humans, which allowed him to run a mile in 73 seconds. Like Spiderman, his healing period from injuries is reduced to hours instead of days. The Super-Soldier Serum is permanent and never wears off making his exposure to gases that would ordinarily overpower others be useless against him.

See how the paragraph compares Spiderman's origins with those of Captain America. We learn what abilities came to them and to what extent. In the next 'body' paragraph, we will compare/analyze their assets. Also, note the length of the paragraph. The day of 5-6 sentence paragraphs is over. The above paragraph took up a page, numbering 251 words, and that is all right. Remember, the 2014 GED Extended Response can be around 900 words (a number suggested due to time constraints, but there is no limit.)

Let's look at the next set of brainstorm ideas from our list, Spiderman and Captain America's assets.

Spiderman	Captain America
As Peter Parker, Spiderman was already very intelligent. He understood and excelled in: - chemistry, physics, biology - engineering - mathematics - his knowledge of science created his webbing A main asset is his subconscious foreseeing sense of danger; this is called his 'spider sense'. It also guides him. Another asset is his 'webbing' to swing from building to building. *(Refer to evidence from article to support your remarks)*	As Steve Rogers, Captain America already had knowledge of: - US military tactics - combat strategy and demolitions - training that made him an expert tactician and field commander - knowledge of judo, western boxing, kickboxing and gymnastics, and after becoming Captain America, he blended them into his own fighting style to become a master in multiple martial arts A main asset is his near-indestructible shield that can be used defensively or thrown as a weapon *(Refer to evidence from article to support your remarks)*

In this 'body' paragraph, we are going to discuss, compare and analyze the assets of Spiderman and Captain America before and after their change. Be sure to pull evidence from the article to support your claims. It might look something like this:

Before Peter Parker became Spiderman, agreeably, he was already brilliant. He excelled in the scientific fields of chemistry, physics, and biology, and he had knowledge of engineering and advanced mathematics. These areas of expertise were what allowed him to create his persona of Spiderman and permitted him to formulate his webbing letting him travel at high speeds "hundreds of feet above street level" from building to building. His "spider sense" guides him in this travel and lets him do this feat with minimal concentration. On the other hand, before becoming Captain America, Steve Rogers was already in the army where he learned military tactics, combat strategy and demolitions. After taking the "Super-Soldier Serum," those accomplishments were heightened making him into an "expert tactician" and "field commander." He became part of the classified Defense Department and later on with Special Ops. Captain America took his army judo and blended it with western boxing, kickboxing and gymnastics until he created his own unique martial arts fighting style. Spiderman has what is called his "spider sense" that alerts him to personal dangers proportional to the severity of the danger. Spiderman's webbing is also a useful asset, but Captain America possesses a near-indestructible shield that he throws with almost unerring accuracy. With it, he can attack multiple targets with a single throw and have the shield return "boomerang-like" to take down an enemy behind him.

Summing It All Up With the Conclusion

The last paragraph is the conclusion. This is the part where you as the writer sum up what has been written. It is where you tie up loose ends and put in closing thoughts, regardless if they have already been expressed. In a nutshell, a good conclusion will:

- Restate the prompt in different words

- Sum up the reasons of whom you chose to support

Below is an example of a conclusion:

Both Spiderman and Captain America represent amazing superheroes. They have unique abilities and assets, both before and after they became their alter egos. However, after comparing and analyzing their capabilities, there is evidence that Captain America is the greater superhero. He has battle strategy at his fingertips, something Spiderman lacks. He also possesses a nearly impenetrable shield. Yes, Spiderman has superior strength and reflexes; he has his spider-sense and can swing from building to building on his webbing, but he does not have the military mind that is honed to outguess an enemy. Spiderman's assets come from science, math and engineering. These do not necessarily help him when he needs to think fast to outsmart a foe. That is why Captain America surpasses Spiderman as the greater superhero.

The Extended Response from Beginning to End

Before going any further, let's put the **prompt**, the **brainstorm,** and then the **extended response** altogether, so you can get an idea of what the whole process might look like. You can also still use the 5-Paragraph Method, but you do not have to.

With that said, below is the prompt. The next page will have the brainstorm outline, and then the entire extended response put together.

Prompt: *Every superhero has abilities and assets that were acquired either before or after the change that made him a Superhero. In your response, analyze the abilities and assets of both Spiderman and Captain America to determine who the greater superhero is. Use relevant and specific evidence from the article to support your response.*

Brainstorm Outline

Introductory paragraph – *Rewrite the prompt* using your own words and decide which side of the argument you are going to support.

	Spiderman	**Captain America**
1st Body Paragraph *Compare and analyze **abilities** in the same paragraph.* *Pull evidence from the article to support your claims as either quotes or paraphrasing.*	Spiderman received abilities when he was bitten by a radioactive spider. Some of them are: - superhuman strength, reflexes and balance - ability to cling to most surfaces - injuries heal in hours	The Super-Soldier Serum enhanced Captain America's metabolic functions. Some of them are: - his endurance, strength, agility, speed, and reflexes grow to the peak of human potential permanently - he is immune to gases and hypnosis - he can run a mile in 73 seconds - injuries heal in hours
	(Refer to evidence from article to support your remarks)	*(Refer to evidence from article to support your remarks)*

	As Peter Parker, Spiderman was already very intelligent. He understood and excelled in: - chemistry, physics, biology - engineering - mathematics - his knowledge of science created his webbing A main asset is his subconscious foreseeing sense of danger; this is called his "spider sense." It also guides him. Another is his 'webbing' to swing from building to building	Captain America had knowledge of: - US military tactics - combat strategy and demolitions - training that made him an expert tactician and field commander - knowledge of judo, western boxing, kickboxing and gymnastics, and after becoming Captain America, he blended them into his own fighting style - he is also a master in multiple martial arts A main asset is his near-indestructible shield that can be used defensively or thrown as a weapon
2nd Body Paragraph *Compare and analyze* **intellect** *in the same paragraph.* *Pull evidence from the article to support your claims as either quotes or paraphrasing.*	*(Refer to evidence from article to support your remarks)*	*(Refer to evidence from article to support your remarks)*

Last paragraph – Restate the prompt using your own words and clarify why the side of the argument you supported was correct. (This essay has 4 paragraphs, and that is okay)

Who Is the Greater Superhero: Spiderman or Captain America?

Captain America and Spiderman are both Superheroes. Both had superior talents and assets before they became Superheroes, and others that were enhanced after their change. Both superheroes also possess abilities that are unique to them, but the evidence shows Captain America's talents and assets outweigh those of Spiderman.

Spiderman, aka Peter Parker, acquired his abilities when he was unexpectedly bitten by a radioactive spider. The result of the bite gave him superhuman strength, reflexes and balance. His overall metabolic efficiency was greatly increased and the "composition of his skeleton, connective tissues muscles and nervous system" were all enhanced until he could dodge almost any attack including "point-blank gunfire." Because of the spider bite, Parker became more spider-like and could crawl across walls and ceilings with fingers and feet that clung to most surfaces. Another benefit is his ability to heal from injuries, including broken bones, within hours. During World War II, Steve Rogers became Captain America because he volunteered to be injected with the "Super-Soldier Serum" and be exposed to a "Vita-Ray." It was an experiment meant to aid the US in its efforts to win the War; the result of these treatments caused Rogers' body to be enhanced to the "peak of human perfection." Though as Captain America, Rogers has no super powers like Spiderman, his strength, endurance, agility, speed, and reflexes were heightened to the "zenith of natural human potential." His new metabolic functions prevented him from feeling fatigue and increased his endurance until he far exceeded ordinary humans, which allowed him to run a mile in 73 seconds. Like Spiderman, his healing period from injuries is reduced to hours instead of days. The Super-Soldier Serum is permanent and never wears off making his exposure to gases that would ordinarily overpower others be useless against him.

Before Peter Parker became Spiderman, agreeably, he was already brilliant. He excelled in the scientific fields of chemistry, physics, and biology, and he had knowledge of engineering and advanced mathematics. These areas of expertise were what allowed him to create his persona of Spiderman and permitted him to formulate his webbing letting him travel at high speeds "hundreds of feet above street level" from building to building. His "spider sense" guides him in this travel and lets him do this feat with minimal concentration. On the other hand, before becoming Captain America, Steve Rogers was already in the army where he learned military tactics, combat strategy and demolitions. After taking the "Super-Soldier Serum," those accomplishments were heightened making him into an "expert tactician" and "field commander." He became part of the classified Defense Department and later on with Special Ops. Captain America took his army judo and blended it with western boxing, kickboxing and gymnastics until he created his own unique martial arts fighting style. Spiderman has what is called his "spider sense" that alerts him to personal dangers proportional to the severity of the danger. Spiderman's webbing is also a useful asset, but Captain America possesses a near-indestructible shield that he throws with almost unerring accuracy. With it, he can attack multiple targets with a single throw and have the shield return "boomerang-like" to take down an enemy behind him.

Both Spiderman and Captain America represent amazing superheroes. They have unique abilities and assets, both before and after they became their alter egos. However, after comparing and analyzing their capabilities, there is evidence that Captain America is the greater superhero. He has battle strategy at his fingertips, something Spiderman lacks. He also possesses a nearly impenetrable shield. Yes, Spiderman has superior strength and reflexes; he has his spider-sense and can swing from building to building on his webbing, but he does not have the military mind that is honed to outguess an enemy. Spiderman's assets come from science, math and engineering. These do not necessarily help him when he needs to think fast to outsmart a foe. That is why Captain America surpasses Spiderman as the greater superhero. (657 words)

The Grading Traits

There are three grading traits in the GED, and each trait has three levels (0, 1 2), 2 being the highest score. Here is a simple overview so you can see how the extended response is being scored and what the grading criteria is. Even a '0' can be scorable, but this is not what you want to aim for.

<u>Trait 1</u> – Creation of Argument and Use of Evidence

Benchmarks Necessary for a Score of '2'

- Gives text-based argument(s) and establishes a purpose that is connected to the prompt

- Brings up relevant and specific evidence from source text to support the argument (It may include a **few** irrelevant pieces of unsupported evidence.)

- Breaks down the issue and/or measures the strength of the argument within the text *(This is the article you read.)* It distinguishes between supported and unsupported claims, and it makes reasonable deductions about underlying premises. It evaluates the credibility of sources.

Benchmarks Necessary for a Score of '1'

- Gives an argument and demonstrates some connection to the prompt

- Brings up some evidence from source text(s) to support the argument and may include a mix of irrelevant pieces or unsupported evidence

- Partially breaks down the issue and/or measures the strength of the argument within the source texts *(This is the article you read)* and may be *simplistic, limited or inaccurate*

Benchmarks Necessary for a Scorable '0'

- May or may not attempt to create an argument *or* lacks purpose or connection to the prompt

- Brings up minimal or *no* evidence from the source text, *(This is the article you read)* and sections of text may be copied

- Minimally breaks down the issue and/or measures the strength of the argument within the article. It may also lack analysis completely because of the absence of understanding

Trait 2 – Develops Ideas, Has Organizational Structure

Benchmarks Necessary for a Score of '2'

The extended response:

- has ideas that are well developed and generally logical; most ideas are detailed

- contains a sensible progression of ideas with clear connections between details and main points

- breaks down an organized structure until it conveys the message and purpose of the response (*This is what you say*) and gives transitional words or phrases between paragraphs

- produces and maintains a formal *style* and appropriate *tone*. STYLE includes longer sentences. You need to state the main points and elaborate on those points. TONE is avoiding exclamation points (!), contractions, abbreviations. Acronyms like NBA (National Basketball Association) are acceptable.

Benchmarks Necessary for a Score of '1'

The extended response:

- contains ideas that lack development, may be simplistic or use vague reasoning

- breaks down some evidence of progression of ideas but detail may be confusing or lack connection to the essay's main idea

- produces an organization structure that does not group ideas well or is partly successful at communicating the article's message

- may use contractions, abbreviations or position in writing to show an awareness of the audience and purpose of the article

- may misuse words and/or choose words that express ideas in unclear terms

Benchmarks Necessary for a Scorable '0'

The extended response:

- has ideas that are poorly or illogically developed, with minimal or no details on main ideas

- has unclear or no progression of ideas and detail may be absent or off-topic with the main idea of the article

- produces useless or no observable organizational structure; it does not apply transitional words between paragraphs or does not do it right

- uses contractions, abbreviations, slang or expresses ideas in unclear terms or repetitious manner

<u>Trait 3</u> – **Clarity and Command of English Grammar, Punctuation, Singular and Plural Nouns** (This section is important as well as long.)

Benchmarks Necessary for a Score of '2'

The extended response:

- establishes mostly correct sentence structure and general understanding that helps clarify writing with regard to the following skills:

  a. Varied sentences are used within a paragraph(s)

  b. Correct use of commas in coordinating conjunctions: *,and ,or ,nor ,for ,but ,so ,yet* when there are 2 independent thoughts on either side of these words (which are called *coordinating conjunctions*). For example: *I need to go to the store**, but** I don't want to drive. The cat ate its food**, so** the dog had to find its own.* If the sentence has one independent thought and then a dependent thought, there is no comma before the conjunction. For example - Martha *bought a new dress **and** wore it to school.*

  c. Correct use of putting a dependent clause before the independent clause and the two are joined by a comma if the dependent clause begins with words such as: *after, although, as, as if, because, before, even though, if, rather than, since, when, where, whereas, wherever, whether, which, and while.* For example - ***While** I was in the shower, the phone rang.*

  d. Parallel structure means using the same pattern of words to show that two or more ideas have the same level of importance. For example - *The production manager was asked to write his report quick**ly**, accurate**ly**, and thorough**ly**.* (The parallel structure makes the *adverbs* flow through the sentence.) *The coach told the* *players that they should **<u>get</u>** a lot of sleep, not **<u>eat</u>** too much, and **<u>do</u>** some warm-up exercises before the game.* (This parallel structure makes all the verbs present tense, which again maintains the flow through the sentence.)

    e. Avoid run-on sentences or fragments. Fragments lack either a subject, a verb or do not communicate a complete thought. An example of the incomplete thought is: *Seeing the boy with the ball* (The fragment has both a subject and a verb but does not communicate a complete thought.)

- avoids making sentences 'too wordy' or 'unclear' and keeps them simple and varied but not repetitious

    ➢ Use transitional words like conjunctive adverbs that support a logical and clear flow in sentences. With conjunctive adverbs, there are 2 independent thoughts on either side of words like: ***<u>;however,</u>***, ***<u>;consequently,</u>***, ***<u>;where as,</u>***, ***<u>;in as much,</u>***. You get the point. For example - *I need to go to the store**<u>; however,</u>** I don't want to drive. The cat ate its food**<u>; consequently,</u>** the dog had to find its own.* Note: a *semicolon* comes before the conjunctive adverb and a *comma* comes right after it.

The following are basic grammar rules the test-taker needs to know.

1. Know homonyms (there vs. their), (to, two, too), and confusing contractions (you're and your, its and it's)

2. Subject-verb agreement (The two must agree to be either singular or plural.) For example: The list <u>of fruits</u> was given to Mary. (When you see 'of', this is a preposition and whatever word(s) is behind it does not decide singular or pluralness. 'List' is the subject and it is singular, so 'was' must be the singular verb. Use plural verbs with two or more subjects when they are connected by 'and'.

3. Be clear with pronouns as to whom or what the words are referring to. A 'thing' cannot be a 'he' or 'she'.

4. Know your capitalization for proper nouns, titles, beginnings of sentences

5. Know how apostrophes are used in possessive nouns. For example: The <u>boy's</u> toy was broken. (The toy belongs to the boy). Note*: Plural nouns DO NOT USE APOSTROPHES.*

6. Know punctuation such as commas, semicolons, and end marks.

7. Essay may contain a few errors in grammar, but they cannot interfere with essay comprehension.

8. Have good spelling habits, but if you don't know how to spell a word, <u>use a different word</u>.

Benchmarks Necessary for a Score of '1'

The extended response:

- the paper might have inconsistent sentence structure; it may contain repetitive, choppy, rambling or awkward sentences that take away from sentence clarity; the writer does not have consistent control over skills (refer to a – e in this trait for a scorable '2')

- has inconsistent control of basic grammar rules (refer to 1-8 in this trait for a scorable '2')

- may have frequent errors in grammar and rules that interfere with comprehension of essay and standard grammar is minimally acceptable for on-demand draft writing (ie) the GED essay

Benchmarks Necessary for a Scorable '0'

The extended response:

- sentence structure is consistently flawed making sentences unclear

- there is minimal control over skills (refer to a –e in this trait for a scorable '2')

- the writer has minimal control of basic grammar rules (refer to 1-8 in this trait for a scorable '2')

- the writer has frequent errors in grammar and rules that interfere with understanding the essay, and standard grammar is unacceptable for on-demand draft writing (ie) the GED essay *or* response is too short to demonstrate level of understanding grammar and punctuation skills

Because test-takers have only 45 minutes to complete the GED essay in the RLA section, there is no expectation that an essay should be completely free of grammar and punctuation errors to receive a score of 2.

Reasons for a Non-Scorable '0':

1. Response contains only text copied from the article or prompt.

2. Response shows no proof that the test-taker has read the prompt *or* it is off-topic

3. Response cannot be understood

4. Response is not in English

5. Response has not even been attempted. (Blank page)

A Few More Tips

- The GED extended response is now taken on computer, there is no more writing on paper

- Watch your time, but be sure to leave several minutes to go over the essay, checking for grammar, misspellings, punctuation problems, etc. (There is *no* spellchecker)

- If it the extended response is too wordy, it is easy to edit it on the computer screen. When time is called, turn it in and relax. The extended response scores for social studies, science and reading/language are usually scored in less than twenty-four hours; however, there can be a backlog due to high volume of test takers and scoring results can take between 2-3 business days. If you have not received email notification by that time, call the GED Testing Service at 1-877-392-6433.

- There are two scores in the RLA. There is the extended response, which will be averaged using the 3 traits; the second score comes from the multiple-choice and drag-and-drop questions from the other section of the test. Together, these scores determine a final score.

- Concentrate on creating an effective essay where evidence is pulled from the article. Show clear organization while moving from point-to-point using adequate, appropriate, and specific details, examples, or reasons *without putting your personal opinion in the content.*

On the following pages are articles and prompts that can be used to write an RLA Extended Response. Read the articles more than once and look for the verb phrases in the prompts that will help you with a brainstorm that utilizes facts from both sides of the argument. Doing this will help you further understand how to write a GED extended response, and do it well.

Also, take what time you need and compose your thoughts, even if the first extended response takes several hours; you might be learning a new skill, so do not beat yourself up! After a few essays, you will begin to understand how everything goes together, and then you will find your essays take less time to write.

When you are finished with an essay, contact an English teacher or someone versed in extended response writing to go over the essay with you and help you understand where your strengths and weaknesses are. Do not throw away your old essays; keep them to look at and see where your previous mistakes were so you do not repeat them. With each successive essay, you will become more at ease with the process. Your writing will be tighter and more professional, and before you know it, you will be ready to take the GED extended response and do well.

SAMPLE ARTICLES

FOR THE RLA EXTENDED RESPONSE

Pros and Cons of Banning Cosmetic Surgery

Prompt – *Cosmetic surgery has become global and is seen by many people as enhancing a person's ability to become more than what they were. Opponents believe it is exploitation to force both men and women to attain an ideal presentation that is far from normal. In your response, decide which viewpoint has the better argument and use relevant and specific evidence from the article to support your response.*

The distinction between cosmetic surgery and other types of surgery, such as reconstructive surgery, is that cosmetic surgery involves techniques intended for the enhancement of appearance. Cosmetic surgery involves both surgical and medical techniques, and it is specifically concerned with maintaining normal appearance, restoring it, or enhancing it beyond the average level toward some aesthetic ideal. Cosmetic procedures have grown dramatically in popularity.

In 2006, nearly 11 million cosmetic procedures were performed in the United States alone, and in 2007, there were nearly 12 million cosmetic procedures performed. That number is over 50 percent higher than 2000 when the number of procedures was just below 6 million.

There is considerable evidence that women's attractiveness is judged more harshly than men's are. In a 1975 study by Adams and Huston, participants were asked to rate the attractiveness of photographs of people of varying ages. The results were that although attractiveness ratings for both men and women declined with age, the rate of decline for women was greater. Researchers report women's magazines have ten and a half times more ads and articles aimed at promoting weight loss than men's magazines do, and over three-quarters of the covers of women's magazines include at least one message about how to change a woman's body appearance by diet, exercise or cosmetic surgery. In Europe, the second largest market for cosmetic procedures, cosmetic surgery is a $2.2 billion a year business. Cosmetic surgery is now also common in countries such as Great Britain, France, and Germany. In Asia, cosmetic surgery has become an accepted practice, and currently it is widely prevalent in China where it is Asia's biggest, cosmetic surgery market.

Proponents for banning cosmetic surgery argue the risks inherent in surgery, not medically necessary, are too great, and that women are merely succumbing to the pressures from men to be beautiful. Allen Ginsburg, a radical writer of the 1960s, said, "Whoever controls the media--the images--controls the culture." He went on further to say the media conveys unrealistic images of the ideal, female body, but women have unique builds and make-up. Ginsburg also pointed out that while the growth in the cosmetic surgery industry enhances peoples' perceptions, it also infers there is something wrong with women's bodies if they don't conform to an ideal, beautiful form.

In contrast, those against the ban of cosmetic surgery argue that women have a right to choose both how they look and by what methods they choose to achieve how they look. They say nobody is forcing anyone to have cosmetic surgery, and that the market is driven by demand. Attractiveness greatly affects first impressions and later on interpersonal relationships.

The freedom to change one's body is important to some women who believe they have historically been regarded as "owned" and "for the use of men." Cosmetic surgery–the ultimate control over one's body–is the latest stage in the emancipation of women and their ability to decide what happens to their bodies. For example, the French performance artist, Orlan, sees plastic surgery as a path towards self-determination. Instead of having her body rejuvenated or made beautiful, she turns the tables. At times, she goes towards the grotesque and uses surgery as a medium for a different project. Orlan designs her body, orchestrates the operations and makes the final decision about when to stop and when to go on. She is the creator, not just the creation.

In a study titled "What Is Beautiful Is Good," psychologists Karen Dion, Ellen Berscheid and Elaine Hatfield asked college students to rate photographs of strangers on a variety of personal characteristics. Those who were judged as 'attractive' were also likely to be rated more intelligent, kind, happy, flexible, interesting, confident, friendly, modest, and successful than those judged unattractive.

Is the Death Penalty a Deterrent in the US?

<u>Prompt</u> – *The article presents arguments from both supporters and critics who disagree about the death penalty's impact on lowering the murder rate in the United States. In your response, analyze both positions presented in the article to determine which one is best supported. Use relevant evidence from the article to support your response.*

Capital punishment is the sentence of death, or practice of execution, handed down as punishment for a criminal offense. It can only be used by a state after a proper, legal trial. The United Nations, in 2008, adopted a resolution calling for a moratorium on the use of the death penalty; however, fifty-eight countries, including the United States and China, still exercise the death penalty. As such, the topic remains highly controversial. Abolitionist groups and international organizations argue that it is cruel and inhumane, while proponents claim that it is an effective and necessary deterrent for the most heinous of crimes.

States believe it is their responsibility to protect the lives of innocent citizens, and enacting the death penalty may save lives by reducing the rate of violent crime. States also say their reasoning is simple; fear of execution can play a powerful, motivating role in convincing potential murderers not to carry out their acts. In an article, "A Sure Way to Prevent Prison Escapes" by Deroy Murdock, he states, "While the prospect of life in prison may be frightening, proponents put forth that death is a more daunting prospect, believing the risk of execution might change the mind of murderers-to-be so that the act is no longer worthwhile for them."

Murdock further states, "The death penalty is the only way to ensure that criminals do not escape back into society or commit further crimes while in prison. While in prison, it is not uncommon for those receiving life in jail sentences to commit homicide, suicide, or other crimes since there is no worse punishment they can receive." He and others believe putting dangerous murderers in prison endangers other prisoners, and the guards who must watch them. Proponents for the death penalty point out another advantage of execution is that it prevents the possibility of an escape from prison. Even the highest, security, detention facilities can have escapees; thus, the only way to be certain that convicted murderers can no longer hurt others is to execute them.

Numerous studies support the deterrent effect of the death penalty, including one from 1985 by Stephen K. Layson at the University of North Carolina. He determined that a single execution deterred 18 murders. Adam Lipdak, in a New York Times article from 2007 wrote, "Another influential study, which looked at over 3,054 counties over two decades, found further support for the claim that murder rates tend to fall as executions rise. In short, the death penalty can-and does-save the lives of innocent people."

However, opponents of the death penalty believe there are many reasons to doubt its deterrent effect. For one thing, they say many criminals may actually find the prospect of the death penalty less daunting than spending the rest of their lives suffering in jail. Amnesty International, in an article titled "Abolish the Death Penalty," said, "Death by execution is generally fairly quick, while a lifetime in prison can be seen as a much more intensive punishment." Furthermore, the article pointed out that even if criminals preferred life in prison to the death penalty, it is not clear that a harsher punishment would effectively deter murders adding, "Heinous crimes often occur in the heat of the moment, with little consideration for their legal repercussions."

Death penalty opponents also state that for a deterrent to be effective, it would have to be immediate and certain. This is not the case with the death penalty cases, which often involve prolonged appeals that sometimes end in acquittals.

Finally, opponents of the death penalty state empirical evidence regarding the deterrence effect is at best mixed. "Saving Lives and Money," a 2009 article by the *Economist*, said that many of the studies which purport to show the deterrence effect are flawed, "…because the impact of capital punishment cannot be disentangled from other factors such as broader social trends, economic factors and demographic changes in a region. Studies have even suggested there is a correlation between the death penalty and higher crime rates. States such as Texas and Oklahoma, which have very high execution rates, also have higher crime rates than most states that do not have the death penalty."

University Education Should Be Free

Prompt - *Nearly every country in the developed world, and more in the developing world, provide free primary and secondary education. Such education is generally accepted as necessary by both liberals and conservatives around the world. In the case of university education, however, there is a great deal of disparity between countries' education policies. In many US states and Europe, students pay fees to attend a university for which they may seek student loans or grants. States often extend financial assistance to individuals who cannot afford to pay fees and lack other payment methods. However, there is a growing belief that a university education should be completely free and considered a citizen's right to attend. In your response, analyze both positions presented in the article to determine which one is best supported. Use relevant evidence from the article to support your response.*

Those who propose a free university education believe it is a fundamental right of individuals to experience a university education and have access to the knowledge it affords. In a 2010 Key Degree article, "How to Reap the Benefits of College," it said, "University offers a huge opportunity. It is a treasure trove of knowledge to be gained and experiences to be had. University provides an opportunity that exists at no other time in an individual's life. It is a time of personal, intellectual, and often spiritual, exploration. In secondary school and in professional life, no such opportunities exist, as they are about instruction and following orders, not about questioning norms and conventions in the same way university so often is." Proponents for a free education also believe attending a university serves as a valuable forum for different views, which everyone has a right to experience if they wish. They believe a life without the critical, thinking tools provided by universities is less full because those without it lack the facility by which to unlock all the doors of perception and knowledge laid before them. Adam Swift, in a 2001 article titled, "Political Philosophy: A Beginner's Guide for Students and Politicians" said, "University experience serves also, in its giving of these opportunities, to shape individuals' views of themselves and society, helping to give form to the relationship between citizen and state on a deepened level. The state has a duty to facilitate this development, as its responsibility includes providing citizens with the wherewithal to take meaningful part in the democratic process." Swift goes on to say that a state can only truly be considered legitimate when an educated electorate approves it; that without a proper education, individuals cannot be effective citizens. Proponents to a free university education believe that in the modern world it is essential to the development of informed citizens.

Opponents to a free university education point out that there is no fundamental right to a university education; it is a service. People should pay for it and not freeload off the taxpayer. Rights exist to provide people with the necessities of life. Opponents point out that some people may never have the "opportunity," like possess the wealth to visit Hawaii, but no one sees states funding every citizen's tropical vacation. Opponents further make a point that even in the presence of fees, there is access to scholarships and loans for people from disadvantaged economic backgrounds to find their way into a university. They add that if people want to take advantage of the networking opportunities available in universities and the employment benefits available to graduates, then they may pay for it.

A student blog in England's newspaper *The Guardian* pointed out that the first year at university sorts the "students from the slackers," and that only a third of students bothered to turn up to lectures. As long as they scrape above the pass rate of forty percent on their end of year exams, they don't care about going to classes. The blog also pointed out that many students believe university life is about alcohol and partying first, and education second. As such, opponents hold it is not the taxpayer's burden to fund that sort of education.

Proponents of free education still argue that a university-educated populace is of great value to any state. They contend it provides extensive economic boons to society. In an article from Ireland's Department of the Taoiseach "Building Ireland's Smart Economy: A Framework for Sustainable Economic Renewal" in 2008, it stated that western countries have a substantial advantage in terms of the production of services and high technology, though this is diminishing gradually as the developing world continues to build up technologically and economically. The Department also cited, "There is a profound advantage to countries that actively promote a culture of 'smart economy'. By facilitating higher education, through state funding of university study, countries increase the likelihood and quantity of investment in their economies by both domestic and foreign firms."

Those in opposition pose a different view saying a highly educated populace does not provide the great economic bounties the supporters of free university education put forth. They point out that countries need educated people, including a certain amount of university graduates, but the idea that everyone having a degree would benefit society economically is unfounded and there are no statistics to prove the other point of view is correct. In 2003, Alison Wolf, wrote a book titled "Does Education Matter?: Myths About Education and Economic Growth" in which she said, "There is no economic benefit when people with degrees are doing jobs that do not require university education, and represents a substantial allotment of resources on the part of the state. Every action has an opportunity cost. If people are willing to take loans to pay for the education that will likely allow them to earn far more than they would without one, then they should be willing to pay for the privilege." She also added that if one is paying for something, it is more likely to be taken seriously.

Should the Legal Driving Age Be Raised to 18?

Prompt - *Should the age of getting a driver's license be raised to 18? Those for and against the change acknowledge the age of the driver and the decisions teens make while behind the wheel are at the center of this controversy in both the US and in Europe. In your response, decide which viewpoint has the better argument and use relevant and specific evidence from the article to support your response.*

The age at which young people can legally drive varies from country to country, but in many places it is lower than 18. For instance, in Alaska, North and South Dakota, Iowa, Montana, Wisconsin, and Wyoming, learners permits are issued to teens at fourteen, but drivers are not allowed to drive from eleven or midnight until six the next morning.

However, as young drivers are the ones seen as most likely to have accidents, mostly from talking or texting while driving, there is a push to raise the driving age to 18. According to the Pew Research Center in a 2009 report titled, "Statistics for Teen Usage of Cell Phones While Driving" it states that despite the fact using a mobile (cell) phone is illegal in many countries, there are a lot of US states where it is completely legal to use a phone even to send text messages while driving. "…indeed one in three texting teens ages 16-17 say they have texted while driving."

This has been identified as a serious problem among teenage drivers who are more familiar with the technology and do not see driving as an environment in which it is inappropriate to divert one's attention. In the past two years, lawmakers in the states of Delaware, Florida, Georgia, Illinois and Massachusetts have discussed raising the legal driving age to 18 because of this problem. These lawmakers believe adding at least a year onto the legal

driving age would bring maturity in all areas and an increased awareness of the dangers of

driving while using mobile media and communication devices. In England, the British

government has also recently considered increasing the driving age from 17 to 18.

Opponents to the increase state this situation should be more a question of experience and

individual adherence to good driving rather than a question of age. According to a BBC News

article from January 2011, "Newry Students Invent Gadget to Stop Dialing Drivers" it states, "If

young people are more likely to be using mobile phones even where it is legal, raising the age

restrictions on driving would not solve the problem. Every year children are becoming more

technologically adept, so it stands to reason that this would simply delay any potential problems

rather than solve them. More resources could be put into the implementation of hands-free

devices, as well as technology, which would prevent people from using phones in the car at all."

Proponents for raising the legal, driving age point out that human life is precious and

while driving remains one of the most dangerous things people do on a day-to-day basis,

governments must do everything reasonable to prevent deaths. In a different BBC News article,

"Is Driving More Dangerous than Flying through Ash?" dated April 2010, after the Icelandic

volcano eruption that grounded many flights in Europe, "Rising the driving age will cut the

number of accidents on the roads. In 2008 alone, in the USA there were 6,428 fatalities involving

young drivers and passengers aged between 15 and 20. Rising the driving age by a year or more

will greatly reduce these accidents and deaths."

Oppositionists agree that young drivers have more accidents, but that is because they are

not very experienced, not simply because they are under 18. Elevating the driving age to 18 or 19

would see these new drivers having more accidents then rather than when they were 16 to17.

Instead, those who oppose the age change suggest the "Pass Plus" plan from the UK that has options like having a more rigorous, driving test or imposing stricter rules on young people even after they have passed the driving test. Supporters say this would help save lives. Advocates say plans of action like the Pass Plus in the UK and Graduate Driver Licensing in the USA could be more widely implemented. Statistics for countries like Finland, where the driving tests are far more advanced, show the positive affects this could have.

Censorship of the Internet

Prompt – *The Internet is growing at a fantastic rate and has become a huge recourse for mass communication and information distribution. This article presents arguments from both supporters and critics of censorship who disagree about the varying degrees of censorship's impact on the freedom of speech. In your response, analyze if you believe governments have the right to censor what is on the web. Use relevant and specific evidence from the article to support your response.*

The Internet can be used to spread information anywhere in the world at a minimal cost due to the increase of computers and other electronic devices in homes. It is one of the most accessible forms of information in the world. However, a growing question is should governments have the right to censor whatever material they see fit; thereby, seizing power over the freedom of information.

Countries that currently censor cultural and controversial Internet sites include China, Vietnam, Pakistan, North Korea, Syria, the United Arab Emirates and Saudi Arabia. This censorship often focuses on seemingly low-risk, social-networking sites like Facebook. While the specific sites banned by countries vary, sites like Facebook are deemed a threat to these countries' internal infrastructure. In the past few years, there has been growing concern over information available on the Internet that could be used to attack or damage society and/or vulnerable individuals.

For example, proponents for censorship state that radical, political opinion websites, including social networking sites, can be used to attack and bully individuals or promote group violence. In recent years, purportedly innocent, social, networking sites have been used to harm others. Victoria Moore, who wrote, "The Fake World of Facebook and Bebo: Suicide and Cyber Bullying" stated that bullies lurked behind the face of having "harmless fun," and Moore added that in some extreme cases, victims of cyber bullying have been led to commit suicide.

Other proponents for censorship point out that both physical and psychological damage have occurred through using social, networking sites because such sites represent a danger to society as a whole and they point out that these sites have become a medium through which others express prejudice, including racism, towards groups and individuals. Proponents also state that if a particular country has a clear religious or cultural majority it is fair to censor those sites which seek to undermine these principles and which can be damaging to a large portion of the population. Proponents for censorship add that governments owe vulnerable citizens the duty of care and believe if governments fail to take the measures required to remove these sites, which would be achieved through censorship, then they (governments) essentially fail their citizens by allowing such sites to exist. Therefore, in censorship advocate eyes, governments have a duty to protect their citizens, and the best way to ensure their safety is censoring such sites.

The BBC News in a report titled, "Teenagers' Poem to Aid Domestic Abuse Facebook Campaign" admitted to a tiny minority of cases of social networking sites being used malevolently, but they point out that social networking sites are also a powerful force for good. The report cited many social, networking pages campaign for the end to issues such as domestic abuse and racism, adding, "Facebook and Twitter were even used to bring citizens together to clean the streets after the riots in the UK in 2011."

Opponents to censorship point out that the situation regarding censorship implies a broader move to blanket-ban areas of the Internet without outlining a clear divide between what would be banned and what would not. For example, censorship opponents ask at what point a website that discusses minority, religious views would be considered undesirable. Would it be at the expression of hatred for nationals of that country, in which case it might constitute hate speech, or not until it tended towards promoting action as in attacking other groups? Opponents to Internet censorship also remark that allowing censorship in these areas could be construed as obstructing the free speech of specified groups, which might only increase militancy against a government or culture who is seen as oppressing the right to an opinion or belief.

Censorship opponents say that outright banning of this kind of prejudice does not directly tackle the problem; instead, it ignores it. They suggest a better way for governments to confront derogatory and prejudicial speech is to engage it in a public forum. There, governments can reasonably point out the flaws and ignorance prejudices embody, rather than desperately try to hide them from public view. In this way, those who are being attacked by these websites would feel as if the government is actively protecting them and their rights while punishing those who have attacked them and those rights. Opponents say that censorship does not solve the problem of prejudice; it simply closes a few websites but allows the offending authors to seek new avenues of broadcasting their message.

Bibliography

"Cosmetic surgery 'needs regulation'." NHS Choices. http://www.nhs.uk/news/2009/ 11November/Pages/ plastic-cosmetic-surgery-botox-filler-warning.aspx (Accessed June 12, 2014)

"Cosmetic Surgery Bargains." http://www.the-cosmetic-surgery-directory.com/ article_bargain.html (Accessed June 12, 2014)

"Cosmetic Surgery." Wikipedia. http://en.wikipedia.org/wiki/Plastic_surgery (Accessed June 12, 2014)

"High Cost of Death Row." The New York Times. (Web), New York, NY. Opinion Editorial September 27, 2009.

"Image is Everything." http://www.exampleessays.com/viewpaper/64950.html (Accessed June 12, 2014)

"Saving Lives and Money." The Economist. Entry posted March 12, 2009. http://muckrack.com/link/cedc/saving-lives-and-money (Accessed June 12, 2014).

Allen, Walter; Epps, Edgar; Haniff, Nesha. 1991. *College in Black and White*. Albany: State University of New York Press. (Accessed June 12, 2014).

Amnesty International. "Abolish the Death Penalty." http://www.amnesty.org/en/death-penalty (Accessed June 12, 2014).

AsiaNews.it. "Internet censorship tightening in Vietnam." June 22, 2010. http://www.asianews.it/news-en/Internet-censorship-tightening-in-Vietnam-18746.html (Accessed June 12, 2014)

BBC News Northern Ireland. "Newry Students Invent Gadget to Stop Dialing Drivers." January 13, 2011. http://www.bbc.com/news/uk-northern-ireland-12181843 (Accessed June 12, 2014)

BBC News. "Driving Age 'Must Increase to 18." July 19, 2007. http://news.bbc.co.uk/ 2/hi/uk_news/politics/6904821.stm (Accessed June 12, 2014)

BBC News. "England riots: Twitter and Facebook users plan clean-up." August 9, 2011, http://www.bbc.co.uk/news/uk-england-london-14456857 (Accessed June 12, 2014)

BBC News. "Is driving more dangerous than flying through ash?" April 21 2010. http://news.bbc.co.uk/2/hi/uk_news/magazine/8633484.stm (Accessed June 12, 2014)

BBC Newsbeat. "Newly Qualified Drivers 'Should be Banned at Night." September 21, 2010. http://www.bbc.co.uk/newsbeat/ 11380399 (Accessed June 12, 2014)

Bennett, Isabella. "Media Censorship in China." Council on Foreign Relations. March 7, 2011. http://sites.asiasociety.org/ asia21summit/wp-content/uploads/ 2010/11/Media-Censorship-in-China-Council-on-Foreign-Relations.pdf (Accessed June 12, 2014)

Black, Ian. "Saudi Arabia Leads Arab Regimes in Internet Censorship." June 30, 2009.http://www.guardian.co.uk/world/ 2009/jun/30/internet-censorship-arab-regimes (Accessed June 12, 2014)

Death Penalty Information Center. http://www.deathpenaltyinfo.org/ (Accessed June 12, 2014).

DeBenedette, Valerie. "Risks of Cosmetic Surgery." November 19 2007. http://www.newimage.com/resource-center/is-plastic-surgery-safe.html (Accessed June 12, 2014)

Department of the Taoiseach. 2008. "Building Ireland's Smart Economy: A Framework for Sustainable Economic Renewal". Government of Ireland. http://www.taoiseach.gov.ie/ BuildingIrelandsSmartEconomy_1_.pdf. (Accessed June 12, 2014).

Dion, Karen, Ellen Berscheid, and Elaine Hatfield. "What is Beautiful is Good." Journal of Personality and Social Psychology. Volume 24, Nov. 3, 1972: pp. 285-290.

Greatrix, Paul. "University Isn't Just a Business—and the Student Isn't Always Right". Entry posted March 14, 2011. http://www.theguardian.com/higher-education-network/higher-education-network-blog/2011/mar/14/students-as-consumers (Accessed June 12, 2014)

Hera.org. "Freedom of Expression." http://www.hrea.org/ index.php?doc_id=408 (Accessed June 12, 2014)

Hill, Christine. 2007. "Still Paying Off that Student Loan". Renee Montagne, (host) Morning Edition (NPR). January 1, 2007. National Public Radio. http://www.npr.org/templates /story/story.php?storyId=6915549 (Accessed June 12, 2014)

"Captain America." Wikipedia. http://en.wikipedia.org/wiki/ Captain_America (Accessed June 12, 2014)

"Spider-Man." Wikipedia. http://en.wikipedia.org/wiki/Spider-Man%27s_powers_and_equipment (Accessed June 12, 2014)

"Texting While Driving." Wikipedia. http://en.wikipedia.org/ August 2011. wiki/Texting_while_driving (Accessed June 12, 2014)

Kiley, Sam. "Terrorists 'May Recruit On Social Networks'." SkyNews. July 12, 2011. http://news.sky.com/home/uk-news/ article/16028962 (Accessed June 12, 2014)

Kita, Nathalie, The history of Plastic surgery. June 23, 2014. http://plasticsurgery.about.com/od/historyofplasticsurgery/ a/history_of_PS.htm (Accessed June 25, 2014)

Klein, Rebecca. "20 Percent Of Teens Don't Graduate High School; Here's What Their Lives Are Like." Huffington Post. Entry posted May 21, 2014. http://www.huffingtonpost.com/ 2014/05/21/why-students-dropout_n_5365949.html (Accessed June 12, 2014)

Liptak, Adam. "Does Death Penalty Save Lives? A New Debate." The New York Times. Web. November 18, 2007. (Accessed June 12, 2014)

Moore, Victoria. "The Fake World of Facebook and Bebo: How Suicide and Cyber Bullying Lurk Behind the Facade of 'Harmless Fun'." August 4, 2009. http://www.dailymail.co.uk/ femail/article-1204062/ The-fake-world-Facebook-Bebo-How-suicide-cyber-bullying-lurk-facade-harmless-fun.html (Accessed June 12, 2014)

Murdock, Deroy. "A Sure Way to Prevent Prison Escapes." Entry posted March 30, 2001. http://www.prodeathpenalty.com/ murdock.htm (Accessed June 12, 2014)

NHTSA. "Teen Drivers-Graduated Driver Licensing." http://www.nhtsa.gov/ Driving+Safety/Teen+Drivers/ Teen+Drivers+-+Graduated+Driver+Licensing (Accessed June 12, 2014)

"Orlan." Wikipedia. http://en.wikipedia.org/wiki/Orlan (Accessed June 12, 2014)

Solent School of Driving. "The Pass Plus Scheme." http://www.solent-driving.com/ id12.html (Accessed June 12, 2014)

Suellentrop, Chris. "How Often Do Prisoners Escape?" Slate. Entry posted February 1, 2001. http://www.slate.com/articles/ news_and_politics/explainer/2001/02/how_often_do_prisoners_escape.html

Swift, Adam. *Political Philosophy: A Beginner's Guide for Students and Politicians.* Polity Press, 2006. Web. http://www.amazon.com/Political-Philosophy-Beginners-Students-Politicians/dp/0745635326 (Accessed June 12, 2014)

Tyjen, Tsai and Paola Scommegna. "U.S. Has World's Highest Incarceration Rate." Population Reference Bureau. Web. August 2012. http://www.prb.org/Publications/Articles/ 2012/us-incarceration.aspx (Accessed June 12, 2014)

Ullman, Ben. 2007. "Should Higher Education Really Be Free For All?" Entry posted January 19, 2007. http://www.newstatesman.com/blogs/campusradicals/2007/01/higher-education-free-students (Accessed June 12, 2014)

United States Department of Statistics. Bureau of Labor Statistics. Web. http://www.bls.gov/news/release/empsit. t04.htm (Accessed June 12, 2014)

Wojtczak, Maria. "Texting while driving: One of the most dangerous habits of teen drivers." November 16, 2010. http://drivingmba.com/2010/11/texting-while-driving-one-of-the-most-dangerous-habits-of-teen-drivers/ (Accessed June 12, 2014)

Wolf, Alison. *Does Education Matter?: Myths About Education and Economic Growth*. 2003. London: Penguin Global. http://www.economist.com/debate/days/view/232

Made in the USA
Las Vegas, NV
27 April 2023

71197706R00037